T0358844

The
A–Z
of
Wellbeing

THE A–Z OF WELLBEING

Text by Becky Bond

An Hachette UK Company
www.hachette.co.uk

Vie Books, an imprint of Summersdale Publishers Ltd
Part of Octopus Publishing Group Limited
Carmelite House
50 Victoria Embankment
LONDON
EC4Y 0DZ
UK

www.summersdale.com

Printed and bound in China

ISBN: 978-1-80007-705-8

Substantial discounts on bulk quantities of Summersdale books are available to corporations, professional associations and other organizations. For details contact general enquiries: telephone: +44 (0) 1243 771107 or email: enquiries@summersdale.com.

The
A–Z
of
Wellbeing

*How to Feel Good
Every Day*

Anna Barnes

vie

Introduction

Welcome to *The A–Z of Wellbeing*. Just by picking up this book you've taken a step in the right direction towards a healthier, happier you.

A sense of wellbeing is how you feel about yourself, other people and your environment. Research shows that people with a higher sense of wellbeing may also benefit from lower levels of disease, stress or injury, be more productive and in some cases, may even live longer. By prioritizing your physical and mental wellbeing, you are also helping the wider community. That's because feeling good – and behaving in a positive way – tends to have a knock-on effect on those around you. Try smiling at someone and you'll soon see that it's contagious!

Let this handy A–Z of tips and suggestions take you to another level of contentment. Be inspired by words from well-known sporting heroes, actors, medical experts and wise thinkers who share their methods of making the most of every day.

From food and fitness to kindness and kissing, each page in this A–Z shines a light on ways to boost your wellbeing. Some advice is short and sweet – a quick tip to raise a smile. Other ideas encourage long-term change. But each offers insight into enjoying your time on this planet in a more fulfilling way.

Everybody's path will be different, but what matters is that you have the courage and the hope to embark on your journey. Use this A–Z to guide you towards a wonderful sense of wellbeing.

is for
Attitude

We all want to feel happy and worthwhile. This is achievable if we learn to approach life with a good attitude, which means being hopeful and optimistic, even in tricky situations. The benefit of having a positive approach towards yourself, those around you, your job, what you eat or how you spend your spare time is that it can boost your sense of wellbeing.

Medical experts believe that the right mindset leaves us feeling more resilient and helps us cope better with stress. As a result, we feel less pressure, our brains are freed up for creativity and productivity and we have a greater chance of finding fulfilment. It also leaves us more space to think about others and their needs, leading to a higher feeling of worth within our social groups.

Research has found that having a good attitude not only aids your sense of mental wellbeing but also plays a large part in boosting your immune system and fighting off bugs.

A positive attitude can also change your perspective. We can all be guilty of feeling envious of other people's lives but it's a pointless exercise. Instead, by learning to accept and feel grateful for what you have and who you are, you'll move closer to an all-round sense of wellbeing.

Make a gratitude list

Take five minutes every day to jot down a few things that have enhanced your life in the last 24 hours. It could be anything – from a song you heard on the radio that made you want to dance, to a tasty sandwich you ate for lunch, a funny meme you saw on social media or a smile from a stranger passing in the street.

By making this a habit, you will slowly start to see the good in more things. Keep hold of the lists you make – perhaps treat yourself to a new notebook – and reread what you have written before you go to sleep and when you wake in the morning. You will soon start to see your gratitude list growing.

You might even want to share parts of your list with people you know. How lovely would it be for a colleague, friend or family member to receive a text telling them that you feel grateful they are in your life? They might even message back to let you know how grateful they are to have you in their life.

Just a few words of gratitude could work wonders for your attitude and lead to a greater sense of all-round wellbeing.

Begin your gratitude list here:

....

....

....

....

....

....

....

....

....

The greatest discovery
of all time is that a
person can change
his future mainly by
changing his attitude.

Oprah Winfrey

A good attitude starts

with gratitude

is for
Balance

There is nothing wrong with cake. There is nothing wrong with lounging on the sofa. And sometimes, there is nothing wrong with simply doing nothing. But too much of any one thing is not great for your physical or mental wellbeing.

Equally, there is a lot to be gained from hard work, keeping fit and using your brain. But if you are always striving to work longer hours, run faster or score higher exam marks, you could burn out, so the key to keeping a healthy mind and body is balance, making time for both work and play.

Of course, it's fine to treat yourself to a big night out but don't leave yourself feeling exhausted by too many late evenings. And yes, answer that one last email out of working hours but avoid turning the behaviour into a habit and learn to truly switch off during your downtime.

Some psychologists believe there are eight areas in our lives that we should weave together for a happy balance: the mental, spiritual, emotional, material, social, physical, professional and pleasurable aspects. Every day does not need to include all of these elements. However, by keeping an eye on each one, and noticing whether there are some playing a larger part than others in your life as a whole, you give yourself a better chance of achieving a balanced way of living, thereby allowing a genuine sense of wellbeing to prevail.

Make a wellbeing wheel

Draw a circle and divide it into eight equal segments. In each segment, write a different element of balance as described earlier: mental, spiritual, emotional, material, social, physical, professional and pleasurable. Then think about your life in relation to that wellbeing wheel. Do you allow yourself enough time to make the most of each element?

It's never too late to start living well

is for
Connection

Feeling like we belong is crucial for our sense of wellbeing. If you're disconnected from those around you, you're more likely to feel isolated and sad. By making time for friends and family – and remaining open to connecting with others – you'll boost your own mood.

There are many ways to make connections. A quick chat with a neighbour can keep you updated about events on your street. Participating in a team sport or group activity encourages camaraderie, while research suggests that belonging to a faith group can improve mental health as it brings you into contact with others with shared beliefs.

Feel-good hormones serotonin, dopamine and oxytocin are released when you connect physically by hugging or holding hands. In fact, clinical evidence points to increased levels of happiness when we shake a stranger's hand.

Astoundingly, connection through touch can also help relieve pain. Think back to your childhood when you fell and grazed your knee. Did a hug help you feel better?

Of course, not everyone likes physical contact, but the good news is that emotional connection is also beneficial for our wellbeing. Empathizing with another's situation can help them feel understood and you feel useful. Keeping yourself connected is a win-win for everyone.

Make new connections

Step out of your comfort zone by meeting new people. Research the social, sporting or hobby groups in your area and pick one that appeals, then take the plunge and go along to the next meeting. Chances are, you leave with a friend or two, and trying something new will give your self-confidence a boost.

Jot down some ideas for new activities to try:

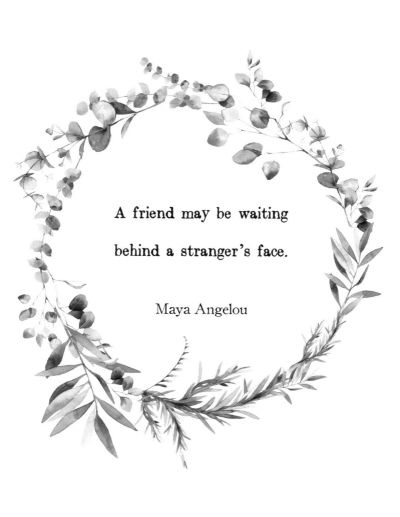

A friend may be waiting

behind a stranger's face.

Maya Angelou

is for
Dance

Humans have danced since the beginning of civilization and the beauty of it is that you don't have to be good at it to enjoy it. Just five minutes of tapping or twirling can lift your mood. Dancing goes hand in hand with wellbeing. By moving your body, you're toning muscles and strengthening bones along with giving your organs a workout as your heart pumps fresh oxygen through your lungs and blood and those feel-good endorphins kick in too.

There are many gifts that dancing can bring. For starters, it's fun. Whether you're shimmying with a partner or performing an impromptu solo around your kitchen, you're sure to be smiling by the time the music stops. Then there's the way it helps us communicate with others, such as a look of love across a dance floor or a nod of understanding during a shared favourite song. Learning steps or hearing a new tune can bring excitement and fulfilment.

YouTube is full of free dance tutorial videos, with many suitable for those with limited mobility, including wheelchair users. All you need to get your wellbeing groove on is great music, a bit of space and a willingness to let yourself be carried away on a wave of good vibes.

Dance like no one's watching

There's no time like the present, so if you're at home, crank up the music and get moving. If you're reading this while commuting, make a plan to get grooving the minute you're back home or maybe you could send a message to a friend to arrange a night out dancing.

To inspire you, write down your five favourite dancing tunes:

1. ....

2. ....

3. ....

4. ....

5. ....

If you're feeling blue, lock yourself in a
room, stand in front of a mirror and dance.

Salma Hayek

E

is for
Eating

The pleasure of eating should never be underestimated. New flavour combinations are exciting, while a familiar, tried-and-tested recipe calms the soul.

It's all too easy to rely on "fast fix" convenience foods but excessive consumption of high-fat and sugar-laden foods can increase the risk of certain health issues. According to the World Health Organization, a healthy, balanced diet allows our bodies and minds to function better, boosting wellbeing.

The good news is that, whether you're vegan, vegetarian, pescatarian, a meat-lover or have an intolerance to some ingredients, eating well isn't hard work. Try to eat at least one high-fibre carbohydrate, such as bread, rice, pasta or potatoes, with each meal, at least five portions of fruit and vegetables each day, cut down on saturated fats, salt and sugar (food labels can help you check these) and drink plenty of fluids – ideally six to eight glasses a day.

Make simple switches such as swapping sugary breakfast cereals for plain natural yoghurt topped with chopped fruit, and topping pizzas with sliced vegetables rather than processed meat.

Enjoying food with others is a fantastic way to socialize. Some families swear by sitting down to eat together and using the time to catch up, while sharing a meal with friends leaves everyone feeling full and fulfilled.

Even if you think your culinary skills are limited, with a bit of planning and practice, it's possible to eat delicious food, which nourishes your body and mind.

Make one new dish every week

Go online or look through recipe books with a focus on health-conscious food. You may be surprised by how appealing they are. In fact, some treats – such as sugar-free banana oatmeal cookies – are even considered to be healthy!

To get in the mood for cooking, put on some feel-good music, set out your ingredients and utensils and focus on the task in hand. The act of creating something is mindful in itself, so even if your dish doesn't go completely to plan first time, the fact that you've given it a shot should give you a sense of pride and boost feelings of wellbeing.

By trying one new recipe every week, you can sample different flavours and practise different cooking skills. After a year, you'll have cooked and eaten over 50 new dishes!

Once you've mastered a few trusted recipes, invite family or friends round to try them out. To minimize stress, make it a casual event. While you're hosting, focus on the satisfaction of sharing something wholesome and delicious, which you have created – food that not only makes you happy but will make your guests smile too.

List your five favourite new dishes here:

1. ....

2. ....

3. ....

4. ....

5. ....

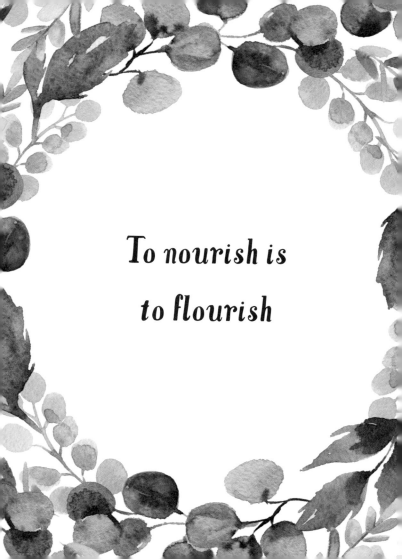

To nourish is

to flourish

To eat is a necessity, but to
eat intelligently is an art.

François de la Rochefoucauld

is for
Family

Families come in all shapes, sizes and make-ups. They can be blood-related, blended, together through fostering, adoption or surrogacy – or a family can be who you have chosen as your tribe, and with whom you know you belong more than anyone else. A family in whatever formation has your back.

Knowing that you're part of a close-knit group of people does wonders for your sense of wellbeing. When you feel valued, loved and protected, you will feel safe to be yourself, to share ideas without prejudice and to be the best version of you.

Being part of a family shouldn't feel stifling and it doesn't mean having to spend every waking hour in a group situation. However, just knowing that your family is there if needed is good for your mental health. Older members of a family group may provide inspiration and wisdom from their own lived experiences. Younger members can bring a fresh perspective.

Make it a priority to check in with family members. Offer to babysit or prepare a meal, but also, think about when they have offered to help you in some way... did you accept that help? By letting another person give something to you, whether it's time, money or a listening ear, you're also gifting them a sense of purpose and wellbeing, which should make you feel pretty good too.

Engage with your family

Take some time to really think about the individual members in your family or group. How are they getting on in life? Are they happy? Could they use some help? Have you seen them enough lately? How could you engage with them more regularly?

Write some ideas in the space below:

Family is not an important

thing. It's everything.

Michael J. Fox

is for
Gardening

Gardening has countless benefits. It improves your strength, helps maintain a healthy heart, boosts vitamin D levels, reduces stress, boosts your mood and helps you sleep better. Plus, if you grow your own fruit and vegetables, you'll be rewarded with nutrient-rich food at your fingertips. It's definitely worth getting your fingernails dirty for!

Another advantage of gardening is that you don't even need your own patch. You can grow flowers, plants and even produce such as potatoes in simple window boxes. Some towns or villages have community allotments where you can enjoy the social side of gardening and share crops.

Being outside in any weather is good for the soul. When you dig in wet and windy conditions, your skin is invigorated with blasts of air and water. In the sunshine, you can take a break and tip your face skyward as the rays relax your tired body. Gardening connects you to the natural elements and can enhance your sense of place and purpose on the planet.

You can also forget about your appearance when you're busy with a spade and trowel. Most gardeners are happy to enjoy the freedom of torn trousers, an old top and muddy boots. Is there anything more freeing than not worrying about how you look?

For a year-round boost to your health and sense of wellbeing, you can't beat getting out in a garden.

Plant your own garden window box

A good start to any gardening project is a conversation with another enthusiast, be it someone you know or a professional at your local garden store, who can advise you on soil, plants and produce. Then when you're all planted up, enjoy watching the contents of your window box blossom over the following months. Make a record of what you've planted here:

Working in the garden gives me something beyond the enjoyment of the senses. It gives me a profound feeling of inner peace.

Ruth Stout

is for
Hydrate

Around 60 per cent of your body and 90 per cent of your blood is made up of water. That's a lot of liquid flowing around inside you. So it's hardly surprising that keeping hydrated is essential for both physical and mental wellbeing.

On average, a person could only live without water for three days because it's needed for almost every aspect of survival. Water regulates your body temperature, aids digestion, lubricates your joints, helps your brain generate certain hormones, removes toxins and is vital for delivering oxygen.

Even mild dehydration can affect your mood, leaving you irritable, anxious and lacking in energy. Your daily recommended fluid intake varies depending on your weight, height and body mass, but health experts suggest that most people need between 1.5 and 2.5 litres of fluid (or six to eight cups) a day, with more needed if you're sweating through heavy work or exercise or in hot weather. Water, lower-fat milk and sugar-free drinks including tea and coffee all count.

An added bonus of upping your water intake is that it improves the appearance and texture of your skin. Also, when drunk before meals, it helps you feel fuller sooner, which can help prevent overeating. By staying properly hydrated, you'll not only feel good but also look good. An easy wellbeing win.

Stay hydrated

Aim to drink the recommended volume of liquid for your body every day. You don't have to stick with plain water though. Providing your drink of choice isn't alcoholic or full of sugar and artificial ingredients, you can keep hydrated with a selection of sugar-free drinks, such as tea, coffee and lower-fat milk. Keep track of your fluid intake for a week with this daily tracker. One box is equal to one glass:

Monday	☐ ☐ ☐ ☐ ☐ ☐ ☐ ☐
Tuesday	☐ ☐ ☐ ☐ ☐ ☐ ☐ ☐
Wednesday	☐ ☐ ☐ ☐ ☐ ☐ ☐ ☐
Thursday	☐ ☐ ☐ ☐ ☐ ☐ ☐ ☐
Friday	☐ ☐ ☐ ☐ ☐ ☐ ☐ ☐
Saturday	☐ ☐ ☐ ☐ ☐ ☐ ☐ ☐
Sunday	☐ ☐ ☐ ☐ ☐ ☐ ☐ ☐

Think of your body
like a car. A glass of
water first thing in
the morning is like
starting your engine.

Joe Wicks

is for
Inspire

Inspiring others to do something good brings its own personal rewards. Imagine how great you would feel if you inspired someone to discover an amazing thing about the world or themselves – it would be a wellbeing double-whammy.

Many teachers train for their profession because they have a genuine wish to inspire children through sharing knowledge and skills. But you do not need to be a qualified teacher to inspire others. Leading by example is an ideal way to show people a new or better way of thinking or acting.

Don't just say you care; ask how a person is, listen to what they have to say and offer advice if it's requested. Demonstrate your enthusiasm for the environment by riding a bicycle to work instead of taking the car. Be open about your own flaws and don't make people look bad to make yourself look better.

Think about all the things you already know or can do. Did you learn these things by yourself or did someone show you? Learning to tie your shoelaces doesn't happen through guesswork, nor does making spaghetti from scratch. Somewhere along the line you'll have been inspired to learn that skill from another.

So, what skills or attributes can you pass on to those around you? Inspiring people to do good or to make choices that create happiness for themselves or others gives everyone involved a little wellbeing boost.

Show what you know

What can you do that might help someone else? How could you share those skills or knowledge for the benefit of others? Is there a family recipe you could show to friends? Can you speak another language, or do you have a party trick? List some ideas for inspiring others here:

I will lead

by example

is for
Jogging

Jogging is the perfect exercise if you want to step up your fitness levels from walking but don't fancy signing up for a marathon. Like most sport, jogging offers great overall benefits for your sense of wellbeing.

Regular jogging can improve your strength, stamina and immune system, as well as releasing a bunch of happy hormones from your brain to keep you smiling. Academic research in Denmark from The Copenhagen

City Heart Study showed that exercise such as jogging could even extend your life – so grab your sports shoes and jog your way to longevity.

Jogging can be done alone, with friends or as part of a club. The beauty of jogging alone is that you can set your own timetable and goals, stepping out of the door any time you want. It gives you a chance to let your mind wander as your feet pound the ground, clearing your head as you go.

If you prefer more structure and need motivation from others, jogging with one or more people might be more your thing. Group chats can be a fun way to spur each other on and celebrate when one of you smashes a personal best. You can also swap ideas on the best kit to use, such as running shoes, sweat tops or tracking apps. Mentally, the first step is always the hardest. But by the end of your first jog, even if you're totally exhausted, you should feel a little wellbeing glow of achievement.

Stretch yourself

Before you start any new exercise, it's important to make sure you know how to warm up and cool down properly. Write out your warm-up and cool-down routines so you don't forget to do them:

The groundwork for all

happiness is good health.

Leigh Hunt

K

is for
Kindness

There are no downsides to kindness. An act of kindness towards another human being can bring them joy, relief and happiness, but that warm fuzzy feeling you get from having helped someone else contributes to your own sense of wellbeing too.

The old cliche "it's better to give than to receive" is backed up by research, proving that being kind to others benefits your quality of life on many levels.

Doing the right thing can ease your own peace of mind and improve your self-esteem. Also, by showing others you care, you're more likely to be treated kindly in the future.

The idea of "paying it forward" is a great one – if someone does a nice thing for you, then you do something nice for a different person.

For example, if a friend bought you a coffee on the way to work, you buy someone else a coffee the next day. Then that person might buy someone else a coffee the day after. So instead of the act of kindness being kept between two people, before you know it, a whole group of people has been treated to a coffee. Kindness is contagious and nobody is immune.

Be kind to a stranger

Make someone smile by doing something kind for them. It doesn't have to be pre-planned or cost anything. Kindness could mean taking five minutes to talk to a lonely person in the park. It could mean helping a stressed mother to carry her heavy pushchair up some stairs. Or you might decide to bake muffins for your new neighbour. Notice how good it feels? Enjoy being kind and reap the wellbeing reward.

It is cool
to be kind

L

is for
Laughter

Have you ever heard anyone say that they don't like laughing? No, because it's one thing that is universally enjoyed by all ages, cultures and creeds. And the best bit? It's great for your mind, body and relationships.

Most people would agree that laughter makes them feel better. A good giggle relaxes your muscles and releases endorphins, taking you out of a negative mindset almost immediately. The added bonus of a cheeky chuckle is that it boosts your immune system. Laughter decreases stress hormones and increases immune cells and infection-fighting antibodies, strengthening your resistance to disease.

Laughter also triggers the release of endorphins, the body's natural feel-good chemicals. In fact, it's so beneficial for mental health that laughter therapy meetings are cropping up worldwide, encouraging people to start the day with a group giggle.

It's also great for building strong relationships with those around us. When laughing with others, you create bonds and common understanding. The memory of a shared laugh with someone can be long-lasting, making it easy to relive the moment and catch the giggles again.

Make time for laughter

There are so many ways to seek laughter. Book tickets for something fun like crazy golf, trampolining or your nearest comedy club. Try laughter therapy or laughter yoga classes – even if the experience doesn't turn out quite as you'd envisaged, at least you'll have a funny story to share with friends later. Focus on things that never fail to raise a giggle, such as your favourite funny TV shows, films, videos or books and make a note of them here, for when you need a laugh:

Laughter is the
best medicine

A day without laughter

is a day wasted.

Charlie Chaplin

is for
Music

Certain melodies have the power to transport your mind to another place or switch your mood in an instant. Up-tempo tunes can get your toes tapping, while calming instrumental music can help you relax.

Humans have been enjoying music for thousands of years, and there's a good reason why our relationship with music has stood the test of time. (The oldest instrument found to date is a 40,000-year-old flute constructed from a vulture's wing, excavated from a cave in southern Germany in 2009.)

Neurological researchers have found that listening to music sparks the release of happy hormones such as dopamine, serotonin and oxytocin, boosting your mood and lowering anxiety.

You might listen to pop songs because they make you smile or to opera because the lyrics fascinate you. There's something out there for everyone and it's impossible to get bored because new musical genres are constantly emerging. Think trip hop, electro-jazz and classical-disco... concepts the Victorians could never have imagined!

Playing an instrument is great for your wellbeing too but you don't have to be the next Mozart. Simply shaking a tambourine to a rhythm is guaranteed to send your spirits soaring. Wellbeing and music are truly intertwined.

Open your ears to something new

However you listen to music – via download, on CD or on vinyl – try listening to a completely different genre or style. Search for music from around the world, old and new and from different genres. Jot down some great new tunes you've heard that made you smile:

Where words fail,

music speaks.

Hans Christian Andersen

is for
Nature

The World Health Organization (WHO) describes nature as our greatest source of health and wellbeing. Nature isn't just about trees and plants but the whole natural environment – our rivers, streams and seas, the earth beneath us, the animals we share the planet with and the unknown galaxies in outer space. By taking an interest in nature and appreciating how it functions, you can feel happier, healthier and more connected to the world around you.

Research has linked daily contact with nature to better health, reduced levels of chronic stress, reductions in obesity and improved concentration. However, living in urban areas can sometimes lead you to forget about the natural world. By stepping away, even momentarily, from shops, neon lights, busy office blocks and traffic, you can reconnect with nature and begin to feel balanced again. Spend your lunch hour in the nearest park and you'll notice your stress levels drop.

Tiny pockets of nature can be created almost anywhere for little wellbeing boosts, such as placing a houseplant on your desk or a bird feeder near a window. You can derive pleasure and satisfaction from simply stopping and observing for a while. Notice which birds start to arrive at your feeder, look at their feathers and their tiny beaks and consider how many other creatures share the universe with you.

Nature opens your heart and mind, helping you to think about the bigger picture instead of focusing on your own worries.

Go camping

The best way to appreciate the natural world is to immerse yourself in it, and what could be more interactive than sleeping – and waking up – in a tent? You don't need to invest in all the kit for your first camping trip as some campsites already have tents pre-pitched, or you could ask friends or colleagues if they can lend you some.

Make it as easy as possible for yourself on your first trip by not going too far or for too long. Try it over a weekend, when it isn't cold or raining and arrange to go with others so that pitching the tent isn't solely your responsibility.

Use your camping trip to focus on reconnecting with nature. Before you go, plan a circular walking route from the campsite, then when you're all pitched up, head out to explore the area. When you return, heat an

easy meal on the stove for an al-fresco dinner under the setting sun.

When you settle down for the night, notice how different everything sounds to when you're at home. With thick walls replaced by canvas, you can hear all that nature has to offer outside – from tweeting birds to the rustling wind. You'll have time to look up at the stars instead of staring at your phone and, without a TV for distraction, you could end up having some great conversations.

Let nature

nurture you

Nature brings solace

in all troubles.

Anne Frank

is for
Openness

Some people instinctively talk openly to those around them, while others prefer to keep their true feelings to themselves, due to shyness, a general need for privacy or a lack of confidence. Small talk has its place in society – it's a great way to get to know new people, for starters. But research has found that deeper, more open conversations are associated with a heightened sense of wellbeing, whether you consider yourself to be an extrovert or an introvert. When you engage in meaningful conversations, you build trust and connections with others, as well as relieve stress.

Talking openly is also important if you find yourself in need of support. You'll instantly lessen your burden by being brave enough to share it, and by allowing someone else to help, you'll be able to take positive steps towards strengthening relationships and building a sense of belonging.

While loved ones may often be able to help you tackle tough situations, it may sometimes make more sense to seek professional help, through talking therapies or support groups. There are groups for practically every difficult life experience such as grief, phobias, abuse, addiction or specific medical conditions. If you're going through it, chances are you're not the first. By being open to sharing your thoughts and receiving help if you need it, you will find yourself taking steps towards a healthier and happier existence and a better sense of wellbeing.

Share something about yourself

Make an effort to have more meaningful conversations with those around you – and have confidence in your own thoughts and opinions. You could choose to share your views about a particular politician, or talk about a long-held desire to go wild swimming. Now is the time to talk to someone you trust. Make a list of those people here:

Speaking your truth is the most powerful tool we all have.

Oprah Winfrey

is for
Pets

From furry cats to scaly reptiles and tiny hamsters to statuesque horses, animals share the world with us and enjoying their company can enrich our lives in so many ways. Pets tick a lot of wellbeing boxes: spending time with them can keep you fit if they need exercising and beat loneliness by bringing you companionship and joy. Pet therapy can even be used as a recovery tool after surgery. Studies prove that spending time with animals reduces anxiety and aids the release of natural endorphins in the brain, making us less sensitive to pain. Research from 2022 claims that 470 million dogs are kept as pets worldwide and there are 370 million pet cats on the planet. We are clearly a global population of pet lovers!

For those without a pet, there are plenty of ways to spend time with animals. A day out at a petting farm is a great way to interact with a variety of species, where you can feed baby lambs, hold a guinea pig on your lap and see piglets suckling. There are now even guided alpaca tours, where you learn more about these interesting animals while leading them on a group walk. Or if you prefer to look and not touch, take a trip to your nearest aquarium and wonder at the underwater world. By simply going on a walk in the countryside and watching cows grazing in a field, you can enjoy a sense of connection with nature and a wellbeing boost.

Care for animals

Just because you don't have a pet doesn't mean you can't spend time with animals. You could offer to take a neighbour's dog for a walk, offer to feed a friend's rabbit when they're away or even lend a hand as a volunteer at an animal shelter.

Take the time to notice the animals all around you in your everyday life too. Sit and watch the birds in your garden, bees buzzing around the flowers or squirrels darting through the local park. By spending time in nature and considering the other creatures sharing your space in the world, you can enjoy a feeling of connectivity to wildlife and the planet, thereby heightening your sense of wellbeing.

Animals are such agreeable friends – they ask no questions; they pass no criticisms.

George Eliot

is for
Quiet

In today's non-stop world, it's rare to experience true quietness of body, mind or spirit. Modern life seems geared towards keeping busy and noise is everywhere. From the ping of an email to the whirr of a washing machine, there's always something in earshot to distract you.

But learning how to switch off from the world and focus on yourself is key to your general wellbeing.

Psychologists consistently extol the virtues of quietude – a sense of stillness, calmness and quiet in a person or a place. Evidence suggests that mastering the art of quietude has many benefits, including encouraging mindfulness, promoting self-awareness, stimulating brain cells, relieving stress, boosting creativity and aiding concentration.

You don't have to aspire to absolute silence though. Natural sounds such as rain falling or birds chirping can be just as calming and good for your senses. You simply need to make time to appreciate these things. Giving yourself ten minutes first thing in the morning to enjoy the peace and put your thoughts in order can get you into the right frame of mind for the rest of the day.

There are many methods for achieving precious moments of peace. Breathing exercises, meditation, yoga, guided imagery or simply sitting comfortably in a quiet room with your eyes closed, can all contribute to your sense of wellbeing.

Moments of morning quiet

Set your alarm ten minutes early. Instead of hitting the snooze button, consider all the things in your life that you're grateful for right now. Then, say a silent thank you, smile and slide into your day with a reassuring sense of wellbeing. Note down the things you're grateful for:

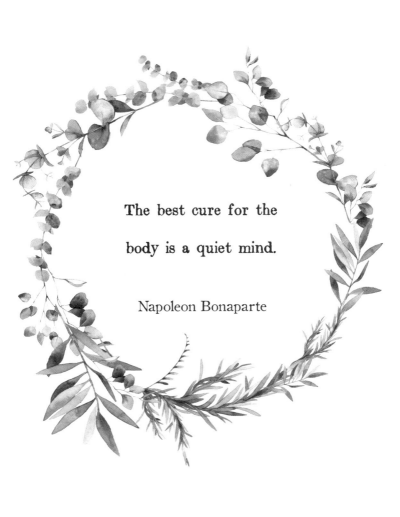

The best cure for the

body is a quiet mind.

Napoleon Bonaparte

is for
Recall

Being able to remember key events or information is a large part of life. Some memories last a lifetime, such as momentous occasions like a wedding or when you encounter particularly deep feelings of grief.

Other memories are short-term and are there to help you retain quick bursts of information that are not needed afterwards. Where did you put your pen?

What's the name of the new person you just met? What time did you agree to meet?

Maintaining a healthy body and mind is a part of nourishing your overall wellbeing. Improving and training your memory is a good way to look after your brain and increase its plasticity over the course of your life.

Most people are reasonably adept at retaining information, but some use memory recall techniques like mind mapping, word games and visualization. Many of these are utilized by some of the best brains in the world – think chess masters and spelling-bee entrants – but these basic methods are available for anybody to learn.

Almost everything you do involves recalling some sort of information. Being forgetful – accidentally missing appointments or struggling to recall the name of an acquaintance – can be frustrating and upsetting. Generally speaking, the better your memory, the more straightforward your everyday life is likely to be, and consequently, the stronger your sense of wellbeing.

Train your brain

Next time you leave the house, make a mental note of ten different things you notice on the way to your destination, quietly counting them on your fingers. If you're walking behind someone, look at what they're wearing. Focus on the colour of their shoes and jacket, if their hair is long or short, curly, straight or non-existent. Take note of sounds you hear too – people chatting, birds singing or music booming through a car window. When you get back home, try and list all ten.

When you've mastered the art of remembering ten things, it's time to up your game. Challenge yourself to 15, 20 or more!

Another test is to watch a movie from start to finish and, without cheating by looking online, try to recall names of minor characters, locations in the story and which actors took key roles in the credits. You could even try this with a friend for fun and compare what you both remember. It's amazing how two different brains can pick up entirely different signals.

Train your memory regularly and you should find the habit of recall spilling into other aspects of your life. At the very least, it might make you a little more observant and the more you know, the more you grow, increasing your sense of satisfaction and wellbeing.

I can do anything
I set my mind to

I always have trouble remembering

three things: faces, names, and — I can't

remember what the third thing is.

Fred Allen

is for
Singing

Whether singing alone in the shower or as part of a choir, belting out a great song has numerous benefits for your mental and physical wellbeing. It can lower stress and blood pressure, improve your breathing and IQ, along with releasing feel-good hormones – and can even help you live longer! It's also great for group bonding.

Is it any wonder then that some historians believe that humans may have been singing from around 800 BC, before we even developed language? It's also no surprise that the type of music around is so varied. Whatever your preferred genre, there will be something you can download or tune into – from country music to rap, hymns or opera, it doesn't really matter. Just open your mouth, take a deep breath and join in.

Not all of us can read music or even sing in tune but that's not the point. After all, karaoke wouldn't be so popular if we only wanted to hear pitch-perfect voices. It's fun watching friends singing their favourite song or taking the microphone to join them for a duet – and when you're having a good time, you're boosting your sense of wellbeing. So don't overthink, just sing.

Sing your heart out

Invite a friend round and pick a musical movie so that you can sing along. Choose one with subtitles, so if you don't know the words to the songs, they're right in front of you. Or book tickets for an interactive sing-along theatre or movie event.

If you're feeling brave and want to go one step further, research local amateur singing groups and turn up for a taster session.

The only thing better than

singing is more singing.

Ella Fitzgerald

is for
Training

Engaging in physical exercise, and training your body, doesn't just keep you supple and healthy, it can also increase your levels of happiness. According to the World Health Organization (WHO), physical activity refers to all movement during both leisure time and work, whether you favour walking, cycling, swimming or a different form of exercise.

Studies have found that physical activity has many benefits, including helping to prevent cardiovascular diseases, cancer and diabetes, reducing symptoms of depression and anxiety, enhancing learning, thinking and judgement skills, ensuring healthy growth and development in young people, and improving overall wellbeing in all ages.

For optimum levels of fitness and wellbeing, most adults should aim for up to 5 hours of moderate exercise or 2 hours 30 minutes of vigorous activity each week. Muscle-strengthening exercises such as squats for stronger legs, the plank for a taut tummy or arm circles for shoulders are also recommended.

Fitness goals can be set for any age group and level of ability but it's always a good idea to speak to your doctor before embarking on a new fitness routine. Joining a gym means that you'll have the support of qualified instructors and may also feel spurred on, working out alongside other gym members. Alternatively, you may prefer to train in the comfort of your home using personal gym equipment or online fitness training videos. Physical training may get you sweating but you'll be rewarded with a glow of achievement and sense of wellbeing after each workout.

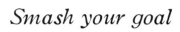

Smash your goal

Pick a fitness goal, whether it's running a 5k, doing 10,000 steps a day for a week or something else. Then plan out some action points to help you achieve it:

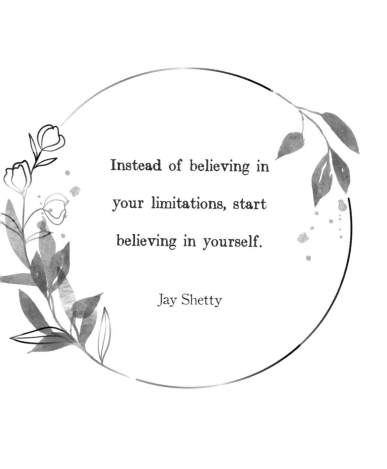

Instead of believing in your limitations, start believing in yourself.

Jay Shetty

is for
Unclutter

When your space is disorganized, it can negatively affect your thoughts and feelings. It's hardly inspiring to wake up to a messy bedroom, piled with laundry. By creating a well-ordered environment, you give yourself a good chance of starting the day in a calmer, happier way. Decluttering experts such as Marie Kondo claim that owning less clutter leaves you with more space, free time and energy for the things you love doing.

However, the thought of making everything neat and tidy in one go can be overwhelming. So how about setting aside an hour to sort through just one chest of drawers? Remove everything and make four piles: keep, sell, donate, recycle/trash.

Be honest about how often you use each item and whether you truly like it. When you have everything in piles, put the "keep" objects neatly in the drawers and see how much space you've created. Remember that what might be clutter for you could be a necessary item for someone else. "Sell" and "donate" goods should either be listed online or passed on to friends or charities. Throw out your remaining items or recycle them.

Looking at a well-ordered, clutter-free space can contribute to your sense of peace, purpose and wellbeing. Also, by selling or passing on unwanted items to others, you could make a bit of money or benefit a worthy cause, which is sure to give you a wellbeing buzz.

Get organized

Remember that almost anything can be tidied – from a small bag to a garden shed – so start small. Make a plan by listing five areas of your space in need of being decluttered and tick them off as you get them looking lovely and tidy.

☐ ....

☐ ....

☐ ....

☐ ....

☐ ....

Life truly begins only after you have put your house in order.

Marie Kondo

is for
Volunteering

By helping others in some way – large or small – you are contributing to society and making the world a better place. Volunteering is something most people can do. You can volunteer your time, money or expertise and the wellbeing benefits for all are far-reaching.

Volunteering is a fabulous way to meet new people, make friends and learn skills, however much spare time you have. Also, whatever your interests, skills and availability, there should be something to suit you. Research has found that volunteering offers many health benefits, including helping you stay physically and mentally active, giving you a sense of purpose and decreasing the risk of depression; it may even help you live longer.

In terms of the effects of volunteering on your sense of wellbeing, it's easier to look at life's bigger picture when you engage with those in need, making you feel grateful for what you have, encouraging empathy and strengthening the place you have within your community.

When volunteering, it's important to ensure that you're well-matched with what you can offer. There are so many organizations crying out for help, such as wildlife or animal shelters, nursing homes, homeless charities, food banks, museums, litter-pick groups, blood banks and schools. If you can think of it, there's probably some way you can help to make the world a better place, and give yourself a wellbeing boost too.

Volunteer your time

Volunteering is a wonderful chance to use your skills to help others. To focus your mind on what you could offer, list some of your skills:

We grow by helping

others grow

is for
Walking

Walking burns calories, tones your legs, makes you feel more energetic and gives you time and space to think. It can contribute to having a healthier heart as well as helping to prevent arthritis in later life. As a form of exercise, it has the power to boost your mood, releasing happy hormones and leaving you feeling more positive. It's easy to incorporate more walking into your day with a few small changes. If you use the bus to commute, get off one stop early and walk the last section. If you drive a car, park a bit further away from your destination. You could also choose to walk up the stairs rather than using a lift.

Some people try to walk 10,000 steps daily and subscribe to apps that monitor their progress. Others join organized walking groups, which are a great way to experience the fun of walking without having to worry about planning a route – the group leader is generally in charge of that. Being part of a walking group helps you forge new friendships as well as upping your step count. Whatever your level, pace or time constraints, a little more walking every day will do wonders for your wellbeing.

Walk your own way

As well as trying to fit in some extra steps during the week, plan to go on a longer walk during your free time – to exercise your body and free your mind.

First, plan a route suitable to your abilities, whether you go for a countryside ramble or a stroll through your nearest city or town. To find routes, look up walks online. Check the weather forecast and plan accordingly, packing sunscreen or waterproofs (or both), and don't forget a map and a fully charged phone. You could also invite a friend or two to keep you company.

To make your walk extra special why not go on a scavenger hunt for interesting items? See if you can spot the following items (you don't have to pick them up – just take a photo or make a note here):

☐ Something beautiful

☐ Something wild

☐ Something that smells amazing

☐ Something that's perfectly imperfect

☐ Something you've never seen before

Write about your finds here:

....

....

....

....

....

If you can't fly then run, If you can't run then walk.

Martin Luther King Jr

Walk wherever your

heart takes you

is for
XXX

Kissing – be it a passionate smooch or a smacker on the cheek from a relative – is great for your wellbeing. It makes both people feel good about themselves and can strengthen the bond between you.

One of the reasons kissing feels so great is due to the flood of happy chemicals released from your brain in the process. It's a classic cocktail of oxytocin, serotonin and dopamine, which combine to make you feel super smiley all over. Kissing also lowers levels of cortisol – the chemical in our bodies that makes us feel stressed.

A good kiss offers various health benefits, such as boosting your immune system and even burning calories – a 4-minute smooch can burn up to 26 calories! Also, just the anticipation of a kiss makes you produce more saliva, which helps create a protective shield on your teeth, preventing the formation of plaque.

Ancient Romans believed that a common cold could be cured by kissing a donkey's nostril, but that's probably best avoided!

Pucker up

If you're in a relationship, set aside more time for kissing – after all, it's fun and free! If you're single, then why not plant a kiss on the cheek of a loved family member or friend – as long as they're happy for you to do this, of course. By making time for more kisses, you'll not only strengthen the bond between you and the recipient, you'll also create mutual feelings of increased wellbeing.

A kiss is a rosy dot placed

on the "i" in loving.

Edmond Rostand

is for
Yoga

Experts believe that yoga has been practised for 5,000 years. Over that time, some techniques may have evolved but the benefits remain, with research finding that yoga improves strength and flexibility as well as easing back pain and arthritis and lowering the risk of heart disease and high blood pressure.

The esssence of yoga is balance. When practised properly, this ancient art not only helps you balance physically but also encourages you to balance your mind by encouraging relaxation, reducing stress and brightening your mood. Many people develop a deep sense of wellbeing when they engage with yoga. It highlights the importance of mindfulness, helping you appreciate where you are "in the moment" as well as promoting physical and mental discipline, perseverance and a sense of purpose.

The teachings of yoga can be applied to other areas of your life too, such as making the most of your relationships and interacting positively with your wider environment.

The World Health Organization (WHO) is so supportive of the practice of yoga for health and wellbeing that they have a yearly International Day of Yoga. People of any age and most abilities can incorporate yoga into their lives and all you really need to get started is a mat and a bit of floor space.

Yoga can be fun too. There are alternative yoga groups such as paddleboard yoga and hot yoga – but it doesn't stop at people! Goat yoga allows you to pet goats while you practise, encouraging human-animal interaction that releases happy hormones and boosts your mood.

Learn a pose

Sukhasana is the basic seated yoga position depicted in historic images of Indian yogis – some of the images are at least 2,000 years old. It's a comfortable pose used traditionally for practising breathing exercises and meditation – ideal if you need to take a few moments to reconnect with your thoughts.

To try Sukhasana for yourself, sit on the floor on a mat or blanket. Cross your legs and place your feet directly below the knees. Press your hip bones down towards the floor and direct the crown of your head upwards to lengthen your spine. Relax your face, jaw and stomach. Breathe deeply through your nose down into your belly.

Yoga doesn't ask you to be more

than you are. But it does ask

you to be all that you are.

Bryan Kest

is for
Zzzz

There's nothing like the feeling of waking up refreshed after a good night's sleep. It helps to prepare you for the day, alert and happy. A healthy sleeping pattern also helps your mind and body to function properly, enhancing your sense of wellbeing.

Advice varies on the amount of sleep you need, but the general consensus seems to fall between seven and nine hours for most adults, although it isn't uncommon for some people to get by with six hours or less.

Lack of sleep prevents your body from recovering and resetting, leading to lower immunity and an increased risk of illness. Also, without sufficient rest, your brain doesn't work as well as it could, increasing forgetfulness and low mood.

Some people are lucky enough to get to the end of the day and then collapse into bed for a solid sleep, but those who struggle to nod off can sometimes end up in a vicious cycle, worrying about their lack of rest and thereby keeping themselves awake.

There are some things you can do to help aid a peaceful night, though. Unwind physically and mentally by switching off all technology 30 minutes before bedtime. Have a shower or bath, ensure your room is dark and avoid caffeine and alcohol. Then simply let your body do the work as you sleep your way to an improved sense of wellbeing.

Create a haven for sleep

By creating a peaceful sleeping environment, you're more likely to feel relaxed and ready to drift off into a restful sleep, giving your body and mind a chance to reset for a great start to the next day.

To turn your bedroom into a sleepy paradise, start by giving it a thorough clean and get rid of mess and clutter. Swap bright lights for gentle low lighting. Check your mattress too – is it still comfortable? If not, consider investing in a mattress topper. Finally, change your bed linen regularly to keep your bed feeling fresh, cosy and inviting.

There is a time for many words and

there is also a time for sleep.

Homer

Conclusion

This A–Z will hopefully have provided you with plenty of inspiration to help you on your way to a happier, healthier, calmer life – all key aspects for an overall sense of wellbeing. Some of the tips and suggestions should be great fun, such as dancing, goat yoga or singing. Others may take you on a journey of discovery – sharing your feelings, volunteering or learning an instrument. But most of the ideas should be approached with an open mind, knowing that not every single one of them will work for you.

As you should now understand, nurturing your wellbeing is a win-win situation. By understanding what it is that makes us human, along with what makes us happy or sad, healthy or unfit (physically and mentally), we give ourselves the best chance of making informed choices, which can benefit both us and our wider community.

After all, what's the worst that can happen by trying something new? At the very least you might learn to laugh at yourself and put an activity on your "done" list, which, in itself, should create a feeling of accomplishment. So – embrace life, seize the moment and choose one of the A–Z suggestions right now to start your journey towards achieving a strong and consistent sense of wellbeing.

Take rest; a field
that has rested gives
a bountiful crop.

Ovid

Smile, breathe
and go slowly.

Thích Nhất Hạnh

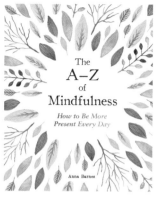

The A–Z of Mindfulness

Anna Barnes

ISBN: 978-1-78783-273-2

Hardback

Squeeze every drop out of each moment and live life to the full by discovering the art of mindfulness. Learn new ways to connect with yourself and the world around you and reignite a sense of wonder in the everyday with this practical ABC of illustrated tips for mindful living.

The A–Z of Positivity

Anna Barnes

ISBN: 978-1-80007-704-1

Hardback

There's magic in making the best out of a bad situation, no matter what life throws at you. Luckily, there are plenty of little things you can do to brighten your outlook and bring a ray of sunshine to every moment. This charming A–Z guide will help your inner optimist thrive, and show you how to bring more positivity into every day.

Image credits

Alphabet – pp.6, 12, 16, 20, 24, 30, 34, 38, 42, 46, 50, 54, 60, 64, 70, 74, 78, 82, 88, 92, 96, 100, 104, 110, 114, 118 © VerisStudio/Shutterstock.com

Background circle – pp.6–7, 12–13, 16–17, 20–21, 24–25, 30–31, 34–35, 38–39, 42–43, 46–47, 50–51, 54–55, 60–61, 64–65, 70–71, 74–75, 78–79, 82–83, 88–89, 92–93, 96–97, 100–101, 104–105, 110–111 ,114–115, 118–119 © Alena Tselesh/Shutterstock.com

Background watercolour – pp.10, 41, 77, 106 © Anassia Art/Shutterstock.com

Cover flowers – pp.2, 21, 59, 87, 117, 128 © Olga Zakharova/Shutterstock.com

Full leaf border – pp.28, 58, 103 © VerisStudio/Shutterstock.com

Gold leaf circle – pp.33, 69, 95, 124 © Net Vector/Shutterstock.com

Hexagon motif – pp.11, 45, 109 © VerisStudio/Shutterstock.com

Leaf corner motif – pp.37, 73, 99, 125 © dolararts/Shutterstock.com

Leaf wreath – pp.19 49 81 113 © Eisfrei/Shutterstock.com

Pink flower motif – pp.15, 53 68 86 © Karma3/Shutterstock.com

Scattered watercolour leaves – pp.4–5, 8, 9, 14, 18, 22, 26, 27, 32, 36, 40, 44, 48, 52, 56, 57, 62, 66, 67, 72, 76, 80, 84, 85, 90, 94, 98, 102, 106, 107, 112, 116, 120, 122, 123 © Nikiparonak/Shutterstock.com

Yellow flower motif – pp.29, 63, 91, 120 © lisima/Shutterstock.com

If you're interested in finding out more about our books, find us on Facebook at **Summersdale Publishers**, on Twitter at **@Summersdale** and on Instagram at **@Summersdalebooks** and get in touch. We'd love to hear from you!.

www.summersdale.com